EXPRESSIONS

RHYTHMICAL THOUGHTS

SUNAAINAA MOHANTY

Contents

Contents

1. LOVE YOURSELF AS NO ONE ELSE WILL

May it be dark or fair,

A chubby girl with curly hair,

Accept the flaws, accept the truth,

For you have the rights to feel the fresh air.

The one you bullied at school,

Is setting examples for the next generation.

The one you called a fool,

Is motivating people to work hard with endless determination.

Ever heard of the word self love?

Yes it says, "to keep yourself happy, that's enough".

You fall for another soul a bit more each and everyday,

But do you accept your imperfections anyway?

Spending hours on social media,

Listen to the latest tracks and groov your legs instead,

Explore some new topics on Google wikipedia,

But leave it! You are maintaining the friendship of your back and the bed.

Prioritize yourself as no one else will,

Love yourself as no one else will.

Live this moment, as the future lies in it,

I add, "live it for yourself", do not wait for anyone else to permit.

2. SELF ACCEPTANCE MATTERS

Do you really need anybody else's acceptance?
Do you really need anybody else's permission to dance?
Do you really need anybody else to give you a chance?
You are gifted with so many talents, just have a glance.
Enlighten your imperfections,
Go beyond all the restrictions,
Spread your wings and fly,
'Am waiting to flaunt your flaws with you', said the blue sky.
Ready to gift chocolates on Valentine's day,
But have you ever gifted quality time to yourself anyway?
You choose to remain silent without any fault,
Then you complain your partner for thr insult,
You spend the whole night about the person who did'nt wish you well at night,
But have you ever closed your eyes and planned your future to be bright?
Accept the way you are!
Omit the jaundiced thoughts that come between your dreams and desires,
Keep the cell phone aside, go to thr terrace and feel the fresh air,
The resulting satisfaction can be felt no where!
I SWEAR!

3. EXPLORE

Explore the colours of the rainbow, Explore the calmness of the winter winds that blow, Explore the cooling shade of the trees that grow, Explore the charm of loving yourself and then see the glow, Explore the shining rays of the sun, Explore your happiness and see others burn, Others burn? Yes when you actually decide to move on, Yes they burn when your life takes a

turn. Indulge yourself into good things, Imagine yourself achieving your goals and living in your dream, Meditate, take deep breaths and the happenings, I add, " none other thsn the Law of Attraction it is". Believing in it, Will help you achieve what you desire, The universe won't disappoint, When you release your vibrstions in the air.

4. WHEN DID I GROW ?

When did I grow ?

Did it happen when things started to bother me ?

Did it happen when I got to know the world changed as Newton sat

under the apple tree ?

Did it happen when I had restrictions and not free ?

Or did it happen when they taught me adukting was just getting a degree

?

When did I grow ?

May be when I learnt isolating myself from others like a pro ?

May be when my mother marked the lost childhood glow ?

Or may be when the situations started to hit me at the meeting of my

eyebrows ?

When did I grow ?

Did it happen when my milk tooth were all gone ?

Did it happen when I pretended as if my stress was none ?

Or did it happen when I walked to the grocery shop all alone ?

With the question marks infront of me,

I miss those days when I was carefree,

The days of joy and happiness,

Never made me feel the word "lonliness".

Caged inside the prison of such thoughts,

To the "still growing" one, 'many battles are yet to be fought',

I, you , we all have to follow the lessons that they have taught,

From an innocent to a matured one, a trap in which we all get caught.

5. BEHIND THE MASK

Realizing the reality,
I wasn't too old to understand the face's variety,
Yes I needed time to clarify the clarity,
When every step of adulting made me discover man's abnormality.
I grew and grew and grew,
Remindind myself every ending was the beginning of a chapter new,
From a circle of giggles and laughs to the smiles of very few,
Getting older was a process of being a hypocrite, I wish I knew.
Pretending is what we do all the time,
Acting to be normal just after committing a crime.
They pretend to be the closest one to you,
Engaged in planning a trap, you will be having no clue.
Each one of us busy in sugar coating task,
Nobody knows what's behind the mask,
Now I guess they taught me being a humbug was the only aim,
Innocence is dead, humanity is dead,
SHAME... SHAME..

6. FROM, TO

From rhymes to anime, series,
From carefree days to the days of worries,
From deciding the flavour of candies to making list of the groceries,
From the united friendships to the unwanted rivalries,
From just adding numbers to finding the derivatives,
From monitoring the class to leading an initiative,
From milk tooth to the permanent ones,
From the shades of pink to the darker ones,
From chloromint to kitkat,
From listening to the stories to the staring at the ceiling and lying flat,
From wearing every piece of cloth to worrying about the layers of fat,
From a guiltless child to a person of who, when,, how and what.

7. APPRECIATE

Appreciate, it may make someone's day, Appreciate, they may need it but won't say, Appreciate, it may help them to shine like the sun in May, Appreciate, it won't harm your status, okay ? Yes they preach of self love, But want me to get rid of my belly stuff, Yes they say 'accept the way

you are', But hate me if I have dark skin and not fair. I don't mind them correcting my mistakes that they see, Faults should be rectified, I agree. You know sand gets hurt by the tide on the shore of the sea, But it still adds to the beauty of the ripples in the blue sea. Keep their imperfections aside for while, Praise what they are and make them smile, Do it genuinely and not like the tears of the crocodile, A little effort by you will help them go a million miles...

8. REALITY

We can't touch,
we can't feel,
What we are
outside is reel,
The desirable
thoughts in our
mind that drill,
Limit our
boundaries and
do not set us
free.

9. CONFESS

Tell them what they mean to you,
Confess how much you love them with
words few,
Whisper in their ear, 'your positivity was
what that drew me towards you',
Help them discover a side of themselves
they never knew.

~SUNAAINAA MOHANTY~

10. LIFE HAPPENED

When I stopped my whys,
When I felt that time teaches something and then flies,
When the pillow was a witness of my screams, my cries,
When I became a diabetic patient of the sweet lies,
When I felt the silence between the lines of poetry,
When I stopped telling my side of the story,
When the wind tangled up my hair, yet felt tranquil,
When peace at the end of the day became the only zeal,
When I realized blue sky is just an illusion,
When the happenings skipped the conclusions.

11. SOMETIMES

Sometimes we regret,

Sometimes we blame our fate,

Sometimes its hard to decide,

Sometimes the decision can not be denied.

Sometimes we are abide by their opinions,

Sometimes we are under our conscious dominion,

Sometimes the choices lead to our destruction,

Sometimes the choices can be reason behind towars us their attention.

Sometimes its fortune's fate,

Sometimes itd our time to rectify ourselves again for the fortune's sake,

Sometimes we need to pull our brakes on the plan we are going to make,

Sometimes the universe has a plan for us, we should take a break.

12. HEY! WILL YOU SPEND SOME TIME WITH ME ?

Something that has never happened before,
Those were the days when the family sat together,
'Hey! will you spend some time with me ?', asked to this generation, the
mother.

Fingers tap and tap and tap for hours,
Life gets pissed off between hashtags, stories and dares,
'Hey! will you spend some time with me ?', asked the fresh air.
Long captions and love quotes that you post,
Putting stories on your anniversary is a must,
But do you think your relationship has love, care, affection and trust ?
No time for the well wishers,
Celebrating birthday with the new comers,
'Hey! will you spend sometime with us ?'
Asked the family members.
I wonder where those days have gone,
Instead of playing with the gadgets,
Children used to play in the streets and have fun,
Love, care, culture and tradition,
Replaced by social media attention.

13. AND NOW ONLY THE WALLS SURROUND ME...

In referrence to the covid19 lockdown....
The days of joy and fun,
The days of busy road and bright sun,
The days of chilling by the shore of the sea,
And now only the walls surround me.
The days of children playing in the garden,
The days when hostellers used to chase the warden,
I miss when we all were mask free,
And now only the walls surround me.
The days when we bargained with the shopkeeper,
The days where virus was away from the news paper,
The days when freedom chose me as its nominees,
And now only the walls surround me.
The days of festivals and functions,
The days when people didnot object the elections,
The days when I was restricted as a devotee,
And now only the walls surround me.
The days of movie dates at home,
The days when I used to have my meals with the family and not alone,
The day has come when I crave for the peaceful hands of my mommy,
And now only the walls surround me.

14. UNNOTICED

Have you noticed ?
Your mom makes an excuse of having a non-photogenic face in a selfie
evertime,
Leaving a space for you, herself standing behind.
Have you noticed ?
Your father wears a sandal which was bought 5 years ago,
He never talks about it,
He just goes with the flow.
Have you noticed ?
Your brother is the only one who annoys you all the time, right ?
But he is the only one who understands you in the battle of life, the real
fight.
Have you noticed ?
The happiness on your sister's face when your dress just perfectly fits to her,
As if it was specially made for her.
Have you noticed ?
The smile of your grandmother,
When she fixes the buttons of your wollen sweater.
Have you noticed ?
Your grandpa's effort when he tries to remember everone's birthday,
Nothing but he just wants to avoid his graying days.

15. SIGHS

The sleepless nights,
Clutch thoughts so tight,
Within me they fight,
Making me choose between what's wrong and what's right,
The nervous stomach aches everytime for voice decides to remain quite,
Unreasonable tears roll down my cheeks and I feel light,
Suddenly I realized everything is a part of the horizontal eight, the
infinite,
Now emotions are the main ingredients in the recipe of life right ?
I wish I could control them just like a knotted kite,
These sleepless nights,
Hold thoughts so tight....

16. A TALE OF A GIRL

Life starts through her,

A blessing she confer,

A pain hard to infer,

With sweet ending to refer.

She gave us life,

She is a daughter, sister and a wife,

She says, 'a gang of five',

Just grabbed her body and pulled her to their side.

A tale of a young girl so pale,

Being brutally raped and killed by the ferocious males,

She began her day with fine sunshine,

And ended with much inhuman pain.

Was that the way to treat ?

When she was out in the street,

Roads covered with long branches of the trees,

She was afraid and not free.

The dresses that she wear,

Are they the reason behind her tears ?

She is blammed more than the culprit,

Why ? because she stepped out of the house at night ?

Long years of independence,

But do you think she is really independent ?

Over lakhs of cases have been filed,

Still no justice for thr victims by the government.

17. I WISH SHE WAS REALLY HOT

I wish I could stop them,
I wish I could punish them,
I wish I could change the laws,

I wish I could change the fear of stepping out where 'getting raped' is the
cause.
Nirbhaya, Asifa, Priyanka and an angel of 180 days,
Yet another case in Hathras,
'Beti bachao beti padhao', is a slogan, warning or a request ?
Candles checked, placards chceked, what's next ?
What is the motive of Beti Bachao ?
If those ferocious ones are going to decide her end ?
'BETA SUDHARO', I wish they could teach their BETAs (sons) to stay
in their boundaries,
And console the angels to relief their worries.
I wish she was really hot,
So everytime when the devil tried to explore her inches,
Burns all over the body,
He would have got.
She has got nice curves, she must be a slut,
She would be asking for it, as she is wearing a mini-skirt,
Brutally raped and murdered and at the end the culprit is her clothes,
From then till now, no change in thelaws.
I repeat "no change in the laws"
The situation is such that even with the relatives she is not safe and free,
No hopes for my nation being a developed country,
Untill and unless her daughters are safe and free.

18. SHE'LL RISE

They will offend her with their words,
They will hurt her with their eyes,
They will kill her for their desire,
But still air she will rise.
Is her freedom a curse ?
Or does it come as a surprise ?
That he dances as she has got diamonds
at the meeting of her thighs.
She is a blend of emotions,
You think she will end herself because of you demons ?

With aggression in her eyes,
Like fire she will rise.
Once, twice, thrice,
After every harassment she cries,
Do not think you'll be escaped after every act,
Like a bird she will rise.

19. STAINS

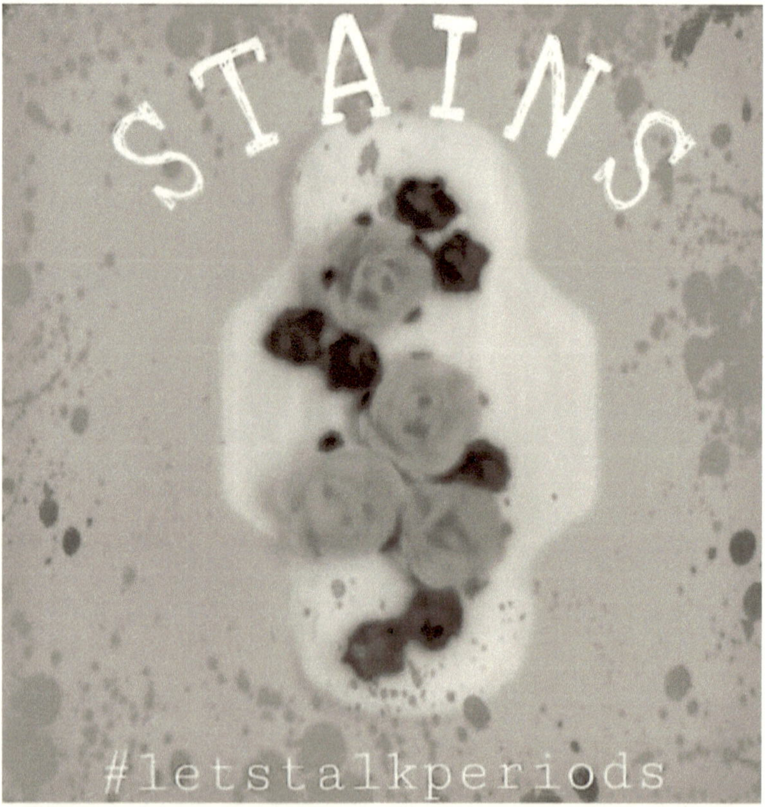

Gifted on this earth capable of conceiving a new soul,
Years passed she crossed a decade,
Adoloscence touched her body,

And those words of restriction that would never fade.
With red stains on the white sheets,
She woke up like the other days,
Unknown to the uniqueness of her gifted body,
For her it was all a mess.
Bleeding for consecutively seven days,
She still has the power to survive the next day,
'Reserving a special term every month,
they bring the painful cramps', she says.
She is strong,
She is powerful,
She faces the critical days,
That would make the opposites, fearful.
The on set and the permanent stoppage,
Something that will never cease,
Yes its all a mess,
But its a masterpiece.

20. AN INDIAN BRIDE

Today her emotions are a blend of shyness and pride,
Today she is going to be someone's bride,
Today the red bangles on her hand and the vermillion on her head,
Depict the love, trust and care for him,
That is never going to fade.
It is the modesty of the bridal veil,
In her promises she shall never fail,
By the glowing flames of the fire pure,
Her virginity will retire.
The glory of steps seven,
Depict that true marriages are made in heaven,
His love and joy is her only goal,
She is the body and he is the soul.
The perfumed flowers on her hair,
Depict the future that she entrust to his care,
Regardless of leaving her surname back,
She holds his hands with much trust and steps to his track.
In her every breath,
Is his fragrance,
He is the essence,
Of her exixtence.

21. CLASSICAL VIBRATIONS

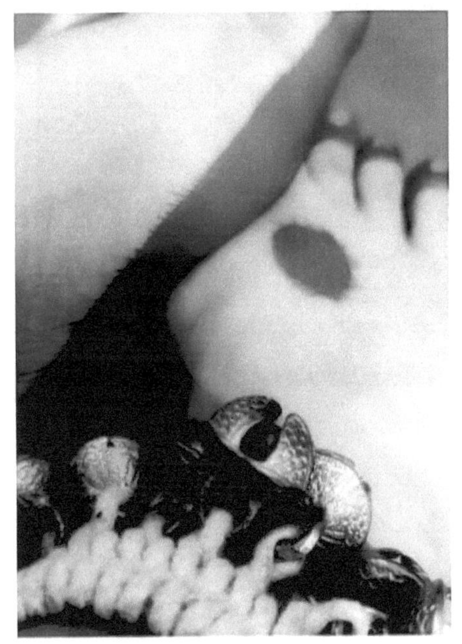

THE GHUNGHROO

THE ODISSI ATTIRE FT. SUNAAINAA MOHANTY (SELF PORTRAIT)

A perfect balance of perfection and beauty,
The attire makes the soul even more pretty,
Look at the consumate Mudras,
The artist is born with it.
Dance is the poetry of the foot,
Where Ghunghroo replicates the heartbeat,

Proud to be born in the land of art,
Depicting a harmonious blend of visual aesthetics.
A crown worn by the females,
Coloured flowers adorned on the bun,
Golden, silver coated jewellery decorated all over the body,
They shine like the gloomy light of the moon.
The eyes express a lot,
Where the lips remain silent,
The sound of the classical vibration,
Causes adrenaline rush inside the classical patient.
A mixture of rhythmic words,
Are insufficient to express the glory of classical dance,
I repeat, 'perfect balance of perfection anmd beauty',
I owe my love towards this Art by showing poetic confetti.

22. THAT RED SEQUIN SAREE

It was the last night of the year,
Everone grooved their legs to the beats of music without any fear,
It was time for everyone to say cheers,
The hands of the clock said 'HAPPY NEW YEAR'.
A red sequin saree it was,
Her curves attracted me over a huge mass,
I still remember the smell of her perfume and wonder of which secretion it
was,
Even Rapunzel would praise her wavy hairs.
The black blouse at the back tied with a string,
The depth of it revealed something,
The contrast of the sequin red and the snowy skin,
AHH! Nothing could match the treat I was getting.
My hands shivered and then my whole body,
I kept my fear aside and got ready,
Collected my courage but still unsteady,
My fingers touched her near the sleeveless cut and I felt like flying already,
And my mind said, " she is the lady".
The conversation was about to start but my alarm screamed,
Sunrays made their way to my skin,
It was so realistic that I could feel blood rushing through my stream,
It was time to unlock my lashes and end my fancy dream.

Note:- This poem is written with the perceptions and imaginations of a male. Sunaainaa has tried to pen down the feelings by altering herselfwith the opposite gender.

• 31 •

23. AN INCIDENT

It was that special day,

Guest were welcomed with flower on the way,
The father was about to say his daughter a Goodbye,
"A typical Indian marriage it is", they say.
Green, yellow and the red attire,
The bridal veil, vermillion and the fire,
Were about to witness the pure bond that they would share,
Living independently in her own house was about to retire.
Then there was a sudden sound at the floral gate,
Everyone cursed the bride's fate,
The pandit said their togetherness was never meant,
Much astonishing was to her the groom's death.
They were about to start a new life,
The incident left her with a mark of the cut with knife,
Everyone expecfted her to live with the tag of 'about to be somwone's wife',
But she broke the stereotype.
His death was never a good sign,
She paid a faultless fine,
Her face appeared as a dull glass of new wine,
But she decided to live like a Sapphire blue stone that shines.
They thought she was lost somewhere,
Yes she was busy joining the oieces of herself that she was about to share,
Searching for happiness anywhere and everywhere,
She met with peace by chasing her dreams and desires.
She lived for her and only her,
Renewed her powers with efforts more,
'Society's talk ?' something that never bothered her,
As lion even gets scared when the lioness roars.

24. SEPARATED

Feelings that once gave serenity to the soul,
Are a reason behind the wet pillows,
Was that taught to me when I was small ?

To fake a smile and hide my sorrows ?
Preaching of love and act so lovingly,
Was what you did,
When it was time to get separated,
You didnot pay any heed.
The moments that we have spent together,
May be then , your feelings were fake,
Today when iI pass through the memory lane,
Makes me feel ssuffocated per breathe I take.
Today when I sit alone and think of you,
Yes, your imitation was what,
That drew me,
Towards you.
Some words are left unspoken,
When I was in favour of love still mistaken,
I have finally stopped writing unrequired letters,
But I wonder how does your existence to me still matters.

25. SHE / HER

She is an open book, yet unopened,
She is a freed bird, yet caged.
She is aware of every happening, yet unaware,
She is frozen water as well the fire.
Hold her hands and she will pen you down in her every poetry,
Try to untangle her hair, she thinks her messy hair is a mystery,
She will wait for you to kiss her forehead,
When after a tiring day she bpretends to be dead.
If you ever meet her,
Take Rose with you she loves the color,
Spray perfume on your wrist, she loves the odour,
Just ask her how was her day to know her more.....

26. STOP BEING SO SILLY

From taking my cooking lessons,

To talking at my back for no reason,

Staring at me from the terrace,

To whitewashing gossips, she never makes a mess,

The one who always keeps an eye on me,

DEAR AUNTIE!

She pretends to be loving me no doubt,

But she will comment on my lipstick, my pout,

She pays more attention to the inches of my heels,

More than cooking her own meals.

She has the super power of noticing the gap between my top and the
bottom,

Her belly folds to three but she is concerned about how many kgs I have
put on,

The one with more than four inches of space between her blouse and the
peticot,

But she is the one who comments on my high waisted jeans and the crop
top.

She is the social butterfly of the colony,

But she will keep a screenshot of my every status in her gallery,

She will be gazing at the guys trying to be friendly,

But will be rumouring aboutbthe guy she saw me with at the fast food
shop,

AUNTIE PLEASE STOP BEING SO SILLY..

27. AND YOU CALLED IT FRIENDSHIP ?

Why did you do this ?
You are not as pure as crystal, master and miss.
You have spoilt everything today,
But that's not going to support your hypocritical sense anyway.
I'll rise someday that's for sure,
Reacting to the rumours today is not a cure,
The fire you have set today will suffocate you someday I assure,
The sparkle on my face that day will be the purest,
I swear.
It must have been easier for you,
The black paint on our friendship that you threw,
Yes they warned me against you,
I regret for ignoring the clues.
Adding spices to a topic is your job right,
You imagine spoiling everything that comes to your eye sight,
I guess you'll come to check if my bedsheet turns red or remains white after
that night,
AAHHAANN! not your faukt, God has blessed you with this talent,
Alright!
Showing off bitchy captions won't make your future bright,
There will be no difference between us if I take the revenge for the fight,

I was a well wisher and will be the same, it may seem a bit dramatic

right ?

But I still pray for your good health and may God lead you right.

28. BITTER TRUTH

True ones stay,
The pseudo bonds find their way,
'Time heals everything', they say,
What about my eyes that filmed the moments of those days ?
Sitting under the gloomy moon by the rippled beach,
Takes me to your trials of ditch,
My fault I skipped the glitch,
Unknotting the bond you were trying to switc.
I had nothing but you,
Today I have everything but not you,
Am glad that the toxicity didn't continue,
But still the thoughts of our togetherness is my heart's only venue.

29. LATE NIGHT QUARRELS WITH THE MOON

Alone in a room after my tiring class,
Alone in a room after my tiring class,
My eyes were in search of the cosy pajamas,
Suddenly the moon attracted me through the French glass,
Nothing but just 'the sky smiling at me' it was.

Rested my back there,
The smile of the sky restricted me to look else where.
Even the crescent moon lighted up my room,
My lips couldn't resist praising the silvery moon.
Me to the beauty:
When You wish to see yourself in the mirror,
The ripples formed by the ocean water,
Lay peacefully, to you they surrender,
Curiously waiting for you to reflect your glamour.

The sun folds for you to breathe,
A love story I witness whenever I retrieve.
The sun sends the cloud as your blanket,
The kind of bond that has retired on this planet.

In your every phase beauty lies,
Steal the night? Ahhan you chose to unveil the beauty of the darkness,
Far away from us yet you make us feel your presence,
I doubt the earthling behavior of easily making anyone feel their absence.

30. THOU / YOU

You are the star that shines above the head,
Let Me lay on You like they rest on the black bed.
I will envelope You like the cloud does to the sky,
I will love You like the eyes love to sleep, till I die.

Your charm is irresistible,
Starring at You, I wish Our lips to staple.
Unconditional tenderness is what I find in your arms,
Rolled upon Your chest my heart beat alarms.

I wish I could seize the time,
When that night Your fingers laced to that of Mine,
A vase, some flowers of love with two glasses of wine,
Oh love! The soulful moments still cause rush in My adrenaline.

31. IS THAT LOVE ?

Is that love?
When under the gloomy moon light,
I close my eyes,
I feel your hands locking me tight,
Then I turn back and notice no one in my eye sight.

Is that love ?
When every video chat ends with an eye contact,
Why? 'Mumma is here', this is the fact.
'I love you' , 'I love you more' fingers tap inside the blanket,
Mumma: 'Have you slept?' and then I lay flat.

Is that love ?
When you dress up like the ice on the mountain,
When you feel the beauty of the sound by the bangles.
When you need your other half like the kite needs air,
When the colour of your skin doesn't matter whether dark or fair.

Is that love ?
When that one phone call adds to your day,
Like the nose pin on a female suits anyway.
When that touch on your waist,
Feels like the heaven is just a step away.

Is that love ?
When our lips locked for the first time,
When you held my hands that night,
When you swiftly clutched me from behind and your lips touched the neck
of mine,
I felt a sizzling feeling of current flowing through my spine.

Is that love ?
When you miss that one person in everyone's presence,
When you recall their body fragrance in their absence,
When you're thankful for that one decision that day and here are it's

consequences,
I am incomplete without you as flower without it's essence,
May God keep us together for the rest of the days.

• 46 •

32. THE GLOWING GREY SPHERE

Silence in the streets,
Starring at the stars, to us the nature's treat,
With the glowing grey sphere the sky is complete,
I wish to visit the place where the ocean and sky meet.

With woollen sliders, pajamas and a cup of cappuccino,
I appreciate the distance or else everyone would fall over like a row of
dominoes,
Unfolding the night, the moon showcases itself as the evening primerose,
Rainbows are aesthetic because the dark sky has the moon that glows.

It hides itself to half and further slims to become crescent,
In every phase it looks attractive yet decent,
Yes am jealous of the thoughts, I heard thoughts travel, to the heavenly
body they went,
Am repeatedly trying my high heels to reach out to you,
O one with stars as friends! Can you reduce the distance between us and
stop making me lament?

33. LOVE IS ONLY A HEARTBEAT AWAY

It gives me butterflies,

It makes me feel the boundless sky,

In the black and white life, it is the dye,

Love? Its only a heartbeat away.

From peeping through the windows,

To praising the spikes of hair when the wind blows,

From looking at the mirror for no reason and feeling shy,

To losing my mind thinking about you the whole day.

Love? Its only a heartbeat away.

I feel so much connected to you,

The happiness is like a child flaunting the dress new.

Crushing over you in my dreams even,

My thoughts just expand like a cake in oven. Am not lying okay?

Love? Its only a heartbeat away.

Damn! My heart beats like any singer's concert today,

Love? Was that, this moment away?

Hey! The one whose vibe has tied me up with you till the present day,

Will you please bloom my life like the Musk rose in May?

34. WE / US

Resting our back under the stars,

Thinking about the love we've made so far.

Praising the slim crescent moon,

Looking at each other we blush like a pink rose in June.

His fingers going through each strand of my hair,

The night sky being the witness of our cozy affair.

Slow instrumental music playing in the background,

Making us feel the color of wound.

Panting, we smooched slowly,

Feeling the warmth, our fingers clutched tightly.

The dark sky, the stars, the moon and some wine,

Cheers baby! Am yours and you're mine.

When am with you the world seems blurry,

Hold my hands forever and I'll pen you down in my every poetry.

35. AND THEY MADE LOVE

And They made love,
Love like it was the last night,
And they made love,
Love like it was the last night
Love like the post fight.

Love like the taste of nectar,

Love like the warmth of a sweater.

And They made love,

Love on the day of full moon and hazy sky,

Love with no 'how' or 'why'.

Love of giggles and smiles,

Love tied them to walk together a million miles.

And They made love,

Love that helped to build each other,

Love like the bright sun during summer.

Love in kissing her neck,

Love as well in talking about life along a lake.

And They made love,

Love in kissing each other at the airport,

Love in being each other's system of support.

Love in believing each other today,

Love that was bound to be cherished for the rest of the days...

36. THE BEAUTY AND THE BEAST

A heart as cold as the poles of the earth,

Roars like a lion, wolf or a gorilla in the dark,

Fell in love with a diva beyond imagination,

Pinch me.. is it a truth or just an illusion?

Fair skin, pink lips and blue eyes,

Her smiles can even shade the cloudy skies,

Her laughter delights the butterflies,

The ocean greets her the moment She passes by.

In forests far and silent,

Her voice is like clear water,

That drips upon stone,

Where Quiet plays alone.

He's a whole new creature,

With fangs and claws,

And hair springing from every pore,

A creature that depicts terror.

A heart that has never known how to love,

Found a shelter to His soul,

She found peace in the cold heart,

And loved unconditionally with Her whole heart.

Her hugs are the petals of the flower rose,

That glows when the dusk is deep,

The garden that closes,

Where Quiet falls asleep.

She can calm him with her kisses,

She can dazzle him with her emerald eyes,

For She is the Beauty,

And He is the Beast.

37. A LETTER

Heart and gift on valentine's day,
Those red rose and
Heart and gift on valentine's day,

Those red rose and chocolates help me say,

I owe my love to you in a special way,

For your love is the reason behind me celebrating this day.

Falling in love with the most unexpected person at the most unexpected
time,

May it be best or worst moment of my life,

You've always stood by me and I don't want to loose you my valentine.
You are my world,

And am the moon,

Am your silent protector,

And night light in the gloom. 'Love at first sight?' Yes I felt that when I
saw you that night,

Black suit and gentleman look,

The next day I started dreaming of you.

The first time when you held my hands,

My emotions made it clear,

For you mean the whole world to me my dear!

I listen to your heartbeat in rhythm with my own,

That warming sound keeps me safe with love you've shown.

You make my life so beautiful,

wonderful, and new.

You're my everything;

I'm so in love with you

38. MY PARTNER IN SLEEP

May it be the day of a bright sun or a night of winter cold,

You lay with me till my eyes unfold,

So smooth you are, together to a posture we mould,

I promise I won't replace you even after you get old.

From the happiest moments to my darkest days,

You have been there for me always.

Nothing can beat my love for you Sweetheart,

Okay! But how can you even tolerate my burps and farts?

How hard my sleep without you would have been!

A nap without you, I can't even imagine,

Heaven is the warmth you provide after you cover my pajamas over the skin,

Peeps! My blanket is what I mean.

39. THE NIGHT

Gazing at the stars under the night sky,

Me and him, him and me, we sigh

,

Words were breathes now,

The handhold, the fresh air, so many things to say but my lips buttoned up,

I don't know why and how,

Silence surrounded us,

It was just like dark sky blooming the white rose,

The night was the calm in the chaos,

Where the shining stars depicted the universe's cheers and applause,

Untying my messy bun he made me face his eyes,

Him to me, "our bodies may die but the bond, the love never dies"

The lines of love and the emotions in between,

It was the non geographical place that I was in,

I rested my head on his shoulder,

(11:11PM)

We wished together we will get older.

40. INFIRMARY SCENES

Some expecting a quick recovery,

Some consoling themselves that there's nothing to worry,

Some heading towards the hospice in a hurry,

Some giving up their lives when to them the world seems blurry.
Some laying on the bed playing the role of a hero,

Some playing with the scissors and forceps like a pro.

Some queuing one after the other in the corridor,

Some thanking the ones in apron for their cure.
Some spending the hours of darkness,

Some playing the supporting role of the patient's.

Some say your turnover can fulfill your wishes,

Some wish a life free of diseases.

41. THANKFUL

They scold us, but teach something new,

Remain silent when they shower their anger with words few,

The words have magic that they say,

Love them Anyway!
God they are,

In human attire,

Their teaching can help you provoke in you the fire,

Your success is their desire.
Conceived by Her,

A blessing she confer,

Trapped in trouble! She is the saviour,

Yes to the first female of everyone's life I refer, The Mother.
All the responsibilities He carries,

Faces the tiring day and smile as if He has no worries,

To fulfil every wish He tries,

Yes the strongest man of the family He is.
Be thankful if you have Them in your life,

Otherwise your value would have been the same as a tree without leaf.

We are adding our days but they are losing theirs,

Let us hold their hands as they held ours,

I repeat "love them anyway",

As the paths will never cross after they release Their last breath in the air

42. BURY ME THERE

Where the ocean and the sky meet,

Where morning sky and the sun greet,

Where patches of greenery stand straight,

Where mother nature holds the cognitive weight,

Where I can draw breath spontaneously,

Where the flesh and blooded ones do not think hypocritically,

Where the soil has no mixture,

Where the sand, slit and clay are perfect by nature,

Where the nestling ones do not fear of the torture,

Where they do not blemish the trees,

Where flora and fauna are the only prompts of poetries,

Where the clouds do not bleed acid,

Where the fumes are invalid,

Where I can smell the petrichor with authenticity,

Where my corpse will serve a sapling with serenity.